PUBLISH
YOUR BOOK
BLUEPRINT
IN 3-DAYS

PUBLISH
YOUR BOOK
BLUEPRINT
IN 3-DAYS

Design & Build Your Book in 10 Easy Steps

DEBORAH S. NELSON

Acknowledgements

Book Cover Design: Omini Graphics

Editorial Consultation: Seaside Services

Proofreading: Sophia Cochran

Interior Build: Alyssa Monique

Dedication

This book is dedicated to the first wave of clients and students who wholeheartedly allowed me to teach them how to self-publish a book. And this book is dedicated to all those who have the same passion!

Cindy White

Audrey Addison Williams

Patty DeDominic

Reverend Maryum Morse

Mannie Jackson

Angela Von Straussenberg

Julia Loggins

Maya Shaw Gale

Joanne Mermis

Suzanne Landry

Joy Hall

John Frederick Feucht

To order additional copies of this book, contact:
www.publishingSOLO.com
or go to Amazon.com

Table of Contents

Introduction

Who is Deborah S. Nelson?

Deborah S. Nelson is the author and publisher of 11 books, including *The Newest Secret, Vacation Rental Owner's Manual, Do-it-Yourself Vacation Rental Branding, The Vacation Rental Travel Guide series, and the Author Your Reality series.* As a publishing coach and curriculum developer, she has guided over 100 authors in publishing their works.

With two decades of experience in the publishing, printing, and advertising industries, it is my passion is to help you get your book to the finish line. This powerful new workbook familiarizes both seasoned and aspiring authors with every step of the digital publishing process. By this workbook or the course end, each author will produce a published proof of their book concept which prepares them for final publication on Amazon.com.

This system not only circumvents countless hours of learning time and frustration, but writers will be well positioned to publish again and again.

Taking the First Step!

Congratulations on taking the first easy step into the world of self–publishing. First let me reassure you that I know what I am doing, and I know how to teach you. I have been in the printing and publishing business for more than 25 years, have self-published a total of 15 books and have helped to teach many first-time authors how to publish multiple books for a grand total of over 100 self-published books.

You may go to www.PublishingSOLO.com and click on videos or library to see what people are saying and to see the many books that have been published through using the curriculum, courses, or private coaching and instruction from Deborah S. Nelson.

Having worked in the traditional publishing and printing business for decades, about 5 years ago, when I discovered and learned about Print on Demand, I jumped into it with both feet, and have never looked back. Just like the historic invention of the printing press brought books and mass education to civilization, Print on Demand and digital publishing has brought another important revolution to the access and distribution of knowledge.

The Self-Publishing Revolution

It is no longer reserved for an elite few to share a skill, an important philosophy, inside perspective, a biography, or a story in published form. Now anyone who knows how to read and write, operate a computer, with Internet service is now able to publish a book and become an author! This is great news, because there is a lot of great information many of us possess to be shared with our circles of influence, even if that is just family and friends, an entire industry, or if the information needs to be shared internationally as a best seller.

The exciting news is that now you can publish you own book using the digital publishing process. Even though it is practically miraculous we can print books digitally almost instantly, publishing a book is not for the faint of heart. It can be complicated, intense, time consuming, and expensive.

If you have always had a passion to write and publish your book, but could not push through the traditional publishing system, you are in luck. And just as likely, you didn't know how to push it through the self-publishing system either. Both systems have their own unique challenges. But we are going to show you how to do it. We aren't just going to tell you, we'll show you! When you are finished following the steps in this manual, you'll have a PROOF COPY of your self-published book idea shipped to you from the digital book publishers.

What You Need

You will need a working computer, a good Internet connection, and a basic knowledge and ability to upload files, save files, and follow instructions. This is the *Do-it-Yourself* version so, if you need further help, please sign up for the online *Publish Your Book Blueprint Course*. This workshop is given personally by Author & Self-Publishing Coach, Deborah S. Nelson. You may also hire

Deborah S. Nelson as your private publishing coach by the hour. You may contact her at dnelson@ publishingSOLO.com

What This Book Includes

There's nothing that compares to hands-on for learning how to do something. Following these instructions will walk you through the basic steps of uploading a book onto Amazon.com. You will *not* publish your final book in this step; but you will publish a book proof and blueprint that will guide you through the process of completing all the steps required to publish a book.

This is a small first step, a "test drive" to show you how to get through the self-publishing process for the first time; one step at a time. We provide you an interior sample book file, which will serve as a blueprint for your final book project. This book is a blueprint, showing the components the proper order of a book. including the front matter, the back matter, and chapter organization and layout. Write in this book to organize all your content for the final publication of your book.

Meanwhile, you will learn how to set up an account with a wholesale print on demand company and upload our perfectly prepared interior book file. You will also create your own book cover using a guided template, submit it all for approval and publish a proof copy of your book.

Options for Your Book Blueprint Project

1 THE DO-IT-YOURSELF GUIDEBOOK

1. Buy the (printed or fillable PDF) version of *Publish Your Book Blueprint in 3 Days*.
2. Read Part I of the book to learn the steps of publishing a book with digital publishing.
3. Use Part II of the book as a guided journal to build your book with all pieces necessary to publish in chronological order. This *blueprint journal* portrays the anatomy of a published book.

COST: Cost of the book, *Publish Your Book Blueprint in 3 Days,* ($39.95 printed and $59.95 for digital PDF Fillable version). This is the least expensive way to learn digital publishing.

2 PRINT YOUR SAMPLE BLUEPRINT

1. Buy *Publish Your Book Blueprint in 3 Days* (printed or PDF fillable version) and read Part 1 and Part II to go through the entire process of printing a self-published *proof* of your book idea.
2. Learn by publishing your own book blueprint, step by step, and set up a print on demand account.
3. Pay a small fee (about $10) for your book blueprint printing and shipping. This option takes you through the digital publishing process in the easiest way possible way, step by step, providing the generic version (generic interior and generic cover) that we included on the Publishing SOLO site at www.PublishingSolo.com/book-blueprint-template.

COST: Cost of the book, ($39.95 for printed, or $59.95 for digital version)plus cost of your blueprint printing and shipping. About $10 in addition to the cost of your printed book.

3 PRINT YOUR CUSTOM BOOK BLUEPRINT

Build a *custom version* of your book concept which includes the name of your book on custom title page, subtitle, author name on the cover and interior of the book. Use your book blueprint to flush out, organize, or to start and finish writing your book in the blueprint journal.

☐ **INTERIOR CUSTOMIZATION**: If you are taking a book blueprint course this is included. If using the do-it-yourself guide (printed or digital version), you may pay an addition $14.95 for our *house designer* to customize your interior, with the name of your book and subtitle on the title pages, author name, headers, and ISBN number.

☐ **COVER CUSTOMIZATION**: If you are taking a *Book Blueprint Course* you will learn how to use the Cover Creator on Createspace and your interior will be customized to match your cover. If using our do-it-yourself curriculum (either printed or digital version); follow the directions for the cover creator at Createspace at no extra cost. In either case, if you want a professional custom cover, you may hire our in-house designer. Go to www.PublishingSOLO.com/book-blueprint-template to download interior files, to start an account on Createspace, or to order custom services. You will prompted to enter a password. Password: ISBN-10: 061592171X

PART 1

PUBLISH YOUR BOOK BLUEPRINT

Chapter 1

Top 10 Most Rejected Bestsellers

How Self-Publishing Saves Time & Rejection

Before starting on your self-publishing journey, I want to share with you my **Top 10 Most Rejected Bestsellers List**. After a multitude of rejections by publishers, these authors went on to sell millions of books! Below are some amazing examples of what I believe to be the biggest advantage to Self-Publishing! Think about all the time and trauma writers have gone through to get their book accepted for publication by a traditional publishing house. Think about it—years and years of submissions and rejection letters.

Dr. Seuss's first children's book was published in 1937. With no Xerox copy machines in existence at that time, he would have typed his original copy, mailed it to a publisher, and then waited for it in return mail, so he could send it out again. This probably took at least 4 years before he found someone to accept his book for publication!

Even up to 10 years ago, a writer is required to mail their manuscript with a self-addressed return envelope and wait for the publisher to read and return it. When I worked inside a publishing house, as the one who read and returned literally hundreds of manuscripts per week, most rejected manuscripts were not returned for 30-60 days!

The following Top 10 Rejected Authors have another story to tell besides the books they have written:

Chicken Soup for the Soul, by Jack Canfield and Mark Victor Hansen was rejected 140 times before published. They were too positive, life affirming, and lacking drama, many publishers said. The public responded well to this encouraging series of books. The Series went on to sell over 143 million copies in 37 languages; and topped every best seller list.

Zen & the Art of Motorcycle Maintenance, by Robert Pirsig, published in 1974, chronicles a 17-day journey across the USA by motorcycle and is a philosophical classic about the meaning of life and the metaphysics of quality. Rejected 121 times—this book has sold over 5 million books worldwide.

Gone with the Wind, one of the most classic romances of all times, by Margaret Mitchell was rejected 38 times, sold over 30 million copies, and won the Pulitzer Prize in 1937. The 1939 movie made of Mitchell's love story, which starred Clark Gable and Vivien Leigh, is the highest grossing Hollywood film of all time; factoring in the value of the dollar at that time.

Dr. Seuss's first children's book called *And to Think I Saw it on Mulberry Street,* published in 1937 was rejected 27 or 28 times according to Seuss; others reported up to some 44 rejections. Seuss has stated that he nearly burned the manuscript before its publication after being rejected by so many publishers. This author later went on to publish 44 children's books for a total of over half a BILLION books sold! He published a book for every rejection he may have received; sweet revenge for him.

Carrie, Stephen King's first book, was rejected 30 times. 'We are not interested in science fiction which deals with negative utopias. They do not sell," one publisher wrote. King did throw it in the trash, but the book was fished out by his wife, and King continued to submit it until it was accepted. A classic in the horror genre, *Carrie* launched King's writing career, and he published some 50 novels which have sold a total of 350 million copies all told.

John Gresham, an author and an attorney, best known for his legal thrillers, submitted *A Time to Kill*, to 14 publishers and 15 agents before it finally published in 1989; for a total of 31 rejections. We have no stats on how well this first novel sold, but as of 2008, John Gresham has sold over 250 million novels.

An epic science-fiction novel, *Dune*, published in 1965, was rejected by 23 publishers before being accepted for publication and selling an estimated 12 million copies. *Dune* is possibly the best science fiction selling book in history, having won the Hugo Award for Best Novel in 1966 and the Nebula Award for best science fiction novel. *Dune* was followed by five sequels. And a film version of the book, starring rock star Sting, remains a cult favorite.

Jonathan Livingston Seagull by Richard Bach, published in 1970, is a prose narrative about a seagull with a passion for flight who explores the joy of flying as a spiritual metaphor. This novella received 18 rejection letters and went on to sell 30 million copies sold worldwide; and was also made into a major motion picture.

Irving Stone's *Lust for Life,* a biographical novel of the life of Vincent van Gogh, received one rejection letter that read, "a long, dull novel about an artist." Once accepted, it later sold 25 million copies, although it was reportedly rejected 16 times.

Harry Potter and the *Philosopher's Stone*, the first in a series of fantasy novels by British author, J. K. Rowling has sold 450 million books in the series. Harry Potter, a fantasy-wizard and main character, has inspired the storyline for some of the best-selling movies of all time. This first book in the series was rejected by 12 publishers. This book series has been published in 67 languages and is likely to be the highest selling book series in history.

Getting to the finishing line is a lot easier with digital publishing. We are thankful for the technology and advances that allow us to be creative without going through this time consuming, ego-crushing submission and rejection process. Sadly, many really great authors and books have been eliminated by this antiquated process.

Chapter 2

Is Self-Publishing Free? Dirty Secrets Revealed

So you think you want to write a book.

What a great dream! I have some encouraging and some truthful news for you. But first, let me tell you why you might want to read this information. I have been involved with self-publishing, or independent publishing for the past 5 years; and prior to that my career was in the printing, publishing, advertising and marketing industries. I ran and owned a small ad agency which specialized in promotional items. Daily, I was involved in imprinting with 85 different printing processes onto hundreds of surfaces including glass, metal, plastics, woods and paper—booklets, brochures, business cards and books. Additionally, I worked for a publishing house for close to 3 years and saw book publishing from the inside perspective. Now I work as a teacher and publishing coach, showing the ropes and inside secrets to clients who want to get through the independent publishing world smoothly, inexpensively, and without frustration or embarrassment!

Therefore, I know the inside scoop on all the printing and publishing processes, both the old and new ways. Let's get to it; the good, the bad, and the ugly of independent publishing industry.

THE GOOD: Self-Publishing's big plus is the lack of rejection letters. Yay! You won't have them; and you won't waste time getting them either! Self-publishing with print on demand is doable and affordable.

THE BAD: Maybe you should have gotten a rejection letter. Now you are published and don't know how to sell your books!

THE UGLY: IT IS NOT FREE TO SELF PUBLSH! It is difficult and time consuming to finally become a published author. There are 3 main steps to publishing a book in physical form: Write the book, Publish, and Sell the book. And it is NOT FREE! Get that out of your head right now. If a self-publishing company tells you it is free, they are misleading you. It may be "free" to sign up for a print on demand account, an ISBN number may even be free, but at some point you are going to have to pay the piper, and that won't be a pretty sight if you aren't prepared.

I tell my clients, writing and publishing your own book is not for the faint of heart. Compared to having a baby, in many ways, it is more difficult. Compare self-publishing to having AND raising a child. It can be expensive, can cause you to lose your mind or if you do not properly plan, you could go broke!

So having said that, publishing a book using print on demand printing is fairly miraculous compared to the days when there was no choice but to go through traditional publishing house and use an ordinary printing press. In fact, it is doable and affordable. Becoming a published author is a dream come true, absolutely exhilarating!

Real Self-Publishing Costs

If you were the general contractor to build you own home, you might choose to "hire yourself" to paint your own walls, tile your floors, or do your own landscaping. As general contractor, you subcontract the pieces that need to complete the entire project. When you are the self-publisher, you will do the same. Many of the processes you may choose to do yourself, such as book cover design, writing your own bio and synopsis or designing your own book cover. Many of these processes require expensive and specialized software, and it is often less expensive and time consuming to hire these pieces done. Many writers do not want to buy the software and endure the learning curve to use it. Some writers are talented in other areas and may already have the software and know-how. It all depends on what skills and resources you may already possess.

Overall, I would say to publish a book professionally without doing any of the pieces yourself, can cost in the neighborhood of 4-7K.

Cost Breakdown of Book Publishing:

1. **EDITORIAL COSTS:** Writing the book is your job. But after it is written, there are three editorial phases your manuscript must go through. These three phases must be done in order! People who are new to publishing tend to lump everything in the first phase and call it "editing." They are three separate phases! First, you will hire someone to edit the content of your book. Hire a content editor who will be sure that absolutely everything is consistent, names and dates are correct, and there is a sensible chronological flow. They will also identify permissions issues to limit any legal issues when you refer to another's name or story. There is no way you can do this yourself, unless you are already a trained editor. Even, then this is difficult because it is not a good policy for a writer to edit their own work. The content edit is a large edit, and it's regarding the structure and content, and making the content clear and understandable.

The second phase is copy-editing. This focuses on the form of the content; such as headings, italics, bold, sizes of fonts, and punctuation. Keep in mind everyone has a different concept of punctuation, and people who have excelled in English can be the worst kind of experts.

This is an ugly area when you are self-published because a lot of people who think they are English experts will inform you of all kinds of punctuation errors. A lot of so-called punctuation "errors" are not really errors. They are simply choices in style. Your copy editor will do this editing according to the style manual of your choice.

The Chicago Manual of Style is a guideline for many periodicals and books, but what style manual you use is your choice. The name of this game is consistency. If you go through the manuscript and make random changes suggested by your cousin who was an English major or your next door neighbor English teacher, you could mess up the consistency and style that your copy editor has previously worked so hard to create.

The third and final part of editorial costs is proofreading. Please! Proofreading is NOT editing! To put it in building terms, would you sand a wood floor after you applied the clear poly coating! NO! So do not edit after your proofread; and do not proofread before you edit! Would you spackle a wall after you paint? No! Do not content or copy edit after you proofread. Stop already! If you use editing and proofreading interchangeably you will create mass confusion among your subcontractors. Additionally, proofreading will be done LAST! Do not proofread prior to content edit or copy edit. This is equivalent to painting a wall in a house you are building prior to plastering the wallboard. Do not put paint on wallboards! You'll just have to do it all over again, after the plaster is applied to the surface. Proofreading is checking for spelling, spacing, and other small typos only! Do this last! No more writing, re-writing, or editing can happen at this point.

EDITORIAL COSTS: Expect to pay a content editor $500-$1500 to edit your book; a copy-editor $150-$500; and a proofreader about $100-$400; depending on the size of your manuscript.

Editorial costs: $750-$2400

2. **COVER DESIGN:** Book cover development is broken down into three book cover phases. The book cover is more important than ever, because about 75% of books are being purchased online and when looking at a book cover online, it can turn into an icon. Book covers can be very tiny when showing up in a shopping cart, so I like to design book covers with super eye catching large graphics.

The old fashioned book cover with blocks of color, in my opinion, looks very corporate and professional, but NOT EYE-CATCHING ONLINE. Do you want to look corporate, professional, or do you want to sell books? The UGLY truth is as independent book authors and publishers, we need to create our own style, and stop copying what has worked for centuries when books were sold in book stores.

The front cover is the most important design element and it must have a LARGE eye catching graphic if you want to sell it online, which is where the majority of books are now sold. The second element of book cover design is the back cover. It will include a SYNOPSIS of the book, the author bio, and the ISBN number. And the third part of the cover design which is not an actual part of the cover, but I like to do it together with the cover is the ABOUT THE AUTHOR. This is because you want the ABOUT THE AUTHOR page to be a longer version of the short author bio written on the back of the book. If you do things in Chronological order, you will save time, money and frustration and keep the project from getting "ugly." In the courses I teach, or with my private clients, we use software templates to "pre-design" the book cover, and when sending to the final graphic artists we pay for only 1 or 2 hours of their time to put the final cover concept into the proper art file form for uploading to your print on demand account.

Book cover design costs: $300-$1500

3. **INTERIOR DESIGN:** Nope-not done yet. This part of the process is equivalent to when you start selecting carpet, paint colors, wall paper, tiles, and other interior decorating touches when building a custom built home. By now you are probably getting a little exhausted and thinking that you are ready to publish. One more process is left. The interior file needs to also be prepared for uploading to the printer. I like to simplify the interior construction into three interior design phases: overall design, image placement, and font/header selections.

What font is going to be used? Happy, sad, simple, educational, professional, childlike? What size is the font? What color are the pages, white or ivory? Do you upgrade the paper? Are there illustrations, photos? Are they black and white or four-color? Do the chapters all start on the right side of the book; do you include study questions at the end of each chapter? What about a Dictionary of Terms at the back of the book, resources, an index, or endnotes? And what do the headings and subheadings look like? What interior design elements such as page dividers, chapter dividers, and other distinguishing design elements can be included to make the interior of the book interesting to read; and consistent with the content and the cover of the book?

These final decisions could drive you crazy, but these kinds of details are what makes a self-published book attractive consistent, and complete. This is what gives 'the look" of your book personality to keep the reader interested.

In my self-publishing courses and private publishing coaching; we complete an interior planner worksheet (and cover planner) which saves a great deal of time for the interior designer. When we turn the manuscript over to the interior book designer, the decisions are already made, and the interior design time is reduced to 25% to 50 %. Interior designers tend to bill by the hour; so this cost can easily go up into the thousands of dollars if you are not prepared before going in!

Interior design costs: $500-$2000

THE FREE PART: The real cost of publishing a book is not FREE, but is more affordable than ever! And the great thing is that no inventory is required. You can purchase a small inventory at wholesale prices, but only if you need copies to sell in person. There are many ways to reduce these costs. One way is to hire people using such services as E-lance, Freelancer. com, 99 designs, etc. There are pitfalls using these services as well. The best thing to do is use some of our pre-planning worksheets, so that you can easily direct the e-lancer, freelancer, or outsourced subcontractor in order to get the best result at the least cost. The Publishing

SOLO Guide includes these worksheets and many tips and tricks how to lead and manage these services for the best result.

Without this knowledge, you may expect to pay an average of $5000 AND UP (more for larger books with more bells and whistles) to prepare your book for a digital print on demand file. Yes. It is 'free" to sign up for a print on demand account. Yes, your book inventory is "free." And yes, the ISBN number may be free (we show you how to get a free ISBN #); but the cost of professionally preparing your book for the digital file will normally cost about $5,000. With Publishing SOLO courses, books, and private coaching you can expect to self-publish for a fraction of that cost. Many of our authors are published for $500-$3000, depending on the size of their book and its complexities. This price includes their self-publishing education. Armed with the do-it-yourself knowledge and new connections, they are lined up to do their next books for even less.

Cost of the Book Blueprint

I invented to Book Blueprint Process to help you really know if you want to self-publish; and if you do, how to actually do it! For $50 you can do-it-yourself with *Publish Your Book Blueprint in 3 Days*. by Deborah S. Nelson) or you can take the course for $297 in a weekend. You leave the course or finish the book with a published Book Blueprint of your book project on the way to you via shipping from the print on demand company.

DO-IT-YOURSELF BOOK BLUEPRINT COSTS:

1. This Book: The cost of this Book; about $39.95 plus shipping

2. Printing & Shipping: The cost of printing your proof through the POD company; about $6-$10 depending on shipping location

3. Customizing your interior to match you book title and ISBN number; about $5 using an interior designer on Fiverr.com

Total cost of printing your own Book Blueprint; about $50-$60.

Chapter 3

Why Become a Published Author?

Before we get started making your Book Blueprint, we want to go through this exercise of identifying why you might want to become a published author.

There are many varied reasons for and advantages to becoming a published author. This is the opportunity for you to fully identify why you want to become a published author. By selecting the top reasons that you are motivated to move through this process, you'll keep these in mind when the going might get a little tough! Check the boxes that apply to you.

☐ **1. Authentic Self Confidence:** When you fulfill your dream to become a published author, expect a surge of self—confidence. This is not the "fake it until you make it," type of self-confidence, but well-earned and authentic. You have articulated your truth, expertise, and your heart to your circle of influence. Creating genuine self-confidence is a boost of momentum to a stalled career, a lackluster social life, or an injured self-esteem. The process of organizing and articulating your expertise, creativity, or personal story, will boost your personal and professional image.

☐ **2. Give Yourself a Raise**: Now that you are a published author, give yourself a raise! Each time you provide a product or service, include a free autographed copy of your book. For example, if you are electrician, and you've written a book: "Do-it-Yourself Wiring for Room Additions," raise your rates 10-20% a few months after most of your clients have been given a copy of the book.

☐ **3. Offer Consulting Services**: As a published author, offer consultation services to create a second income or additional income to your existing business. Consultants and coaches often charge a minimum of $100 an hour for their guidance, expertise, and experience. With a published book in your field, your knowledge can save novices thousands of dollars with access to your industry resources, connections, and your experience of knowing "how not to do something!"

☐ **4. Speaking Engagements:** Becoming a best-selling author is not always the end game of being published. Speaking engagements can bring in fees from a small stipend to unfathomable amounts. Even just speaking for free at a local event, can allow you to sell your books at the back of the room, and bring in a few hundred dollars for just a few hours of your time. Most speaking agencies and bureaus require that you are a published author before accepting you in their speaker's portfolio.

☐ **5. Leverage Your Books:** Once you used print on demand for your publishing method; you may buy your books wholesale directly from the printer for a fraction of the retail price. Give your books to charity, for a tax write-off for the retail amount, or give your books away at seminars, public events, workshops, as a very inexpensive way of marketing your services.

☐ **6. Book Sales**: Sell your books from your website to create an additional income stream. Over 73% of books are now being purchased online. It is not necessary to make your books available in book stores to become a successful author anymore. This is the old model of publishing, and the digital model of publishing moves books online, not through bookstores. For local sales, you may also set up a table at local business events, book fairs, or industry wide fairs to find new clients. While making book sales, you will offset the cost of the booth.

☐ **7. Workshops & Events:** Use your book at the curriculum for workshops and events that you set up at your place of business; or locally at an establishment that will appreciate the niche traffic your class or workshop will bring to their place of business. These events can be free (with book sales as the money earner) or you can charge a fee to the participants. This is a marketing opportunity to upsell consulting or coaching services, or your regular business services. You are the expert at the front of the room; and your services will practically sell themselves in this environment.

☐ **8. Celebrity Status**: As a published author, you are in a celebrity class. Even if only 100 people read your book, you will be seen as a local celebrity. Be sure to enhance your Facebook, Twitter, Google Plus, and your dating profiles with your author status! People are impressed with published authors; and rank you with a higher status in social circles. You'll get invited to exclusive events, parties, and dinner parties. Be sure to brush up your hairstyle, dress, and personal ambiance when attending these events. Remember to bring a few copies of your books in case you meet someone you want to give an autographed copy of the book.

☐ **9. Media Publicity:** Harvest the opportunity to share your knowledge, wisdom, creativity, or expertise on local or national radio or television. It is up to you how far you want to take the momentum of becoming a published author.

☐ **10. Establish Your Own Publishing Company**: Some people get so excited about becoming an author, they start their own independent publishing company. Once you get one book published, many others start to form. You may publish audio books, e-books, kindle books; and translate your books into other languages to market in other countries. Knowing how to use digital publishing makes it fairly easy to start an independent publishing brand; to that, you may publish many other works inexpensively and begin to develop a following for your body of work.

☐ **11. Advertising Vehicle:** Many people in business publish a book to share their knowledge; and include special offers in the back of the book to attract new business.

☐ **12. Leaving a Legacy:** Many people want to publish a book solely to leave a legacy. There is no amount of money that can offset the value of sharing a life of experiences, images, and wisdom with a generation yet to come. The ability to write and publish such a book affordably is priceless and generates the most profit of all; a legacy of love left for those who remain behind.

You Don't Have to Be a Best Selling Author to Be a Successful Author!

Becoming a best-selling author is the desired model of success produced by the traditional publishing company model. The need to publish at least 25,000 books (to make each book affordable), and to sell multitudes of books in order to be profitable, perpetuates the glamorization of the best-selling author profile.

With digital and print on demand publishing being affordable ("from free"-$3k per book to build the digital file, and no inventory required); no one has to be a best seller! Success becomes a matter of leveraging your author status to increase your income, exposure, expertise, and creativity to whatever is your desired circle of influence.

Do not let well-meaning friends and family define what a successful author is for you! Identify why you want to be an author and what kind of author you want to be before going on this journey. When people ask you potentially judgemental and embossing questions such as *So, just how many books have you sold?* You will be prepared with a good come back. If you know what your purpose is in being an author, you can answer proudly (for example):

> *"My book is not necessarily about book sales. Since I have become a published author, my consulting business had added $20k income per year to my bottom line."*

However, if you want to be a best-selling author, there is no reason why you can't be one. Amazon.com has produced a multitude of best-selling authors, to rival any top authors coming from the traditional publishing model. On demand book printing has changed the way the book publishing industry functions and now you, too can become a part of the digital publishing era.

Chapter 4

Am I Qualified to be an Author?

Before we get into actually making your book, we need to address "that elephant in the room." Most all of my students who decided to publish their book, had doubts about their ability to become an author. Some had bad memories of red marks on their papers given by English teachers in high school or college. Some just doubt that their story is interesting, powerful, or unique. Yet something continues to move them to write! I want to reassure you that most people have doubts about their writing. I don't doubt anyone. If you know how to read and write, have a PC and Internet connection, you can publish you book. I believe that everyone has a story to tell, and if they are moved to share it, writing and publishing is a great way to reach out to those who need and want to hear their story.

Difference between a Writer and an Author

A writer is someone who writes a lot. Maybe you write in your journal weekly, monthly or even daily. Or maybe you are working on a novel and are in the habit of writing. An author is someone who actually gets their works published and is able to share them with others.

Conquer Your Fear

This workbook is designed to take you step by step through the process of publishing a book blueprint in 3 days. By creating your book concept and book cover, and going through all the steps to get it published, you will see that it is possible to move from being a writer to a published author.

A Story to Tell or Perfect Writing Skills?

If I asked you which is more important as an author—perfect writing skills or a story to tell, what would you think? I remind writers every day that what makes a true writer is what they have to say. If you don't have anything to say, it does not matter how well you say it! Think about all the great tools we have available now, from spell check, to grammar check, and even sentence structure is built into some of the software. We can hire content editors, copy editors, and proofreaders. If you have a passionate story to share, a skill people want to learn about or an important system of living to teach, by all means, do not let spelling or a nit-picky English teacher from your past be a roadblock. If you have something to say, and you love to write, let's get started with your BOOK BLUEPRINT right away!

Different types of Authors

With all types of people in the world, there are all types of authors. Some people want to become a best-selling author with their name in lights and their books in the front areas of bookstores. In essence they want to be a full time author, travelling, and speaking, and giving radio and television interviews. They want to make a living at being an author and nothing less will do. I say, go for it!

Some authors want to enjoy the creative experience of publishing one book, and others want to write and publish a book as a legacy to their families. Still yet, there are those who have showcased their artwork in a four color book. One of my students, Sophia Cochran, published a book of about a dozen of her own paintings, with a description of each painting as spoken by the subject of the painting. This was an amazing compilation of her works. She is an artist and enjoyed writing the pieces as they related to the story of her artwork. Her grown children were given a copy of the book and this book created an extra special bridge and bond that was unexpected.

Many of my students find that once they complete the publishing process for the first time, the water fountain of books is turned on. Some are writing their 3rd and 4th books now. One of my students who is amazingly talented and creative, put a book of poetry together which she had been working on for 20 years. Her clients and business associates see this accomplished counselor in a whole new light.

Many people are entrepreneurs or professionals and want to write a book in their field. This boosts their credibility and expertise, opening the doors for speaking engagements in their industry, and the opportunity to be hired for consulting. Becoming an author in most cases increases your social status, and professional status.

Chapter 5

Publish A Custom Book Blueprint

Your Copyrights

Before we get started I want to go over copyrights. The beauty of self-publishing is that you own all the rights to your intellectual material. That means no one can claim any part of your royalties as they all belong to you.

Most print on demand and self-publishing companies clearly state that your copyrights belong to you. Here is a statement from Createspace about copyrights:

> "YOU and you alone own the copyright and ALL rights to books published through Createspace. At anytime, you can withdraw your work from publication and publish elsewhere, or, you can simultaneously publish through other outlets. The one small issue is the ISBN. If you get a Createspace ISBN, you can only use it to publish with Createspace. To publish anywhere else, you will need to buy your own. That decision depends entirely on your future plans and doesn't need to be made right now."

Copyrights that Belong to Others

When you publish anything for public consumption be very aware of any intellectual property that may belong to others. Seriously consider the legal and ethical implications when you use someone else's material. Even if it is a quote, or a story, you'll want to get the exact quote, and for written permissions to use their story. If using photos or illustrations, be sure you have purchased them from the creator, and be sure you have the proper permission to publish their work in your book. In addition, you will also give credit to any original works that are included in your book.

There are a multitude of print on demand companies, but I recommend using Createspace for a number of reasons.

1. Createspace is the wholesale print on demand arm of Amazon.com and offers an automated transition from publishing to sales. Once your book is printed with Createspace it becomes automatically available on Amazon for sale; unless you stop it.

2. Createspace offers free and custom ISBN numbers. This is a simple process compared to other print on demand companies.

3. Customer Service at Createspace is the best. They have a calling system which is toll free, and inexpensive if you live internationally outside of the US and Canada. With a lot of automated systems, they have blended them with a very human touch.

About Digital Glitches

This is a do-it-yourself workbook and I have made every effort to simplify the digital publishing process, but systems change, software updates, and errors can occur on the printer's end. If you run into glitches, contact Createspace; they are excellent and available on the telephone. If you find the do-it-yourself process too difficult, join us for an online workshop where all your questions may be answered personally by me.

You may also sign up for one half hour free publishing coaching consultation with Deborah S. Nelson; but this session is for help with your book vision and not to be used as a help desk for digital publishing questions.

☐ **STEP 1**: Understanding the Book Life Cycle.

In this step here are a few simple definitions of the anatomy of a how a book comes to life.

☐ 1. Write the book

☐ 2. Publish the book

☐ 3. Market the book

Many people have a manuscript or two "sitting around," in a drawer or computer file. But most get stuck at the publishing the book stage, because the traditional publishing industry accepts very few books for publishing. Tradition publishing houses are looking to publish "**A** Authors," which include celebrities, politicians, and well-established authors. Receiving hundreds of rejection letters does not sound like most people's idea of a good time. Steven King received hundreds of rejection letters before his books were accepted for publication; and it very likely took a couple of years to get through that part of the process.

In recent years, traditional publishers only accept "*A* Authors," which means the author is already popular, and they know their investment will return. So for us "unknowns" and first time authors, the traditional publishing route is all but impossible.

Writing the book can be a challenge as well. I am going to help you get through that stage by teaching you the very simple basics of uploading a "sample book blueprint" to Amazon.com.

This 'blank book template" is powerful. It will become your specialized journal to help you organize and complete your book project. I am providing the technical files for you to upload, and your Book Blueprint will be the launching pad for you to run through the self-publishing process, and create a place to finish writing your book's content. As you write and organize your book's interior details, you will learn about all the components necessary to complete a book.

Now you know that there are three phases to bringing a book to life: Write the book, publish the book, and finally, market the book. Not all books need to be a best seller. If you write a book on the art of tatting, it will only appeal to a certain audience. If you write a book on basic electrical wiring it will only appeal to those who need this knowledge. Do not every underestimate what you know. There are plenty of people who do not know what you know.

☐ **STEP 2**: The Basic Book Components.

Let's learn about the main components of a book.

☐ 1. The Interior Design: The interior design includes the front matter, the body and content of the book, and the back matter. The front matter contains such items as dedication, preface, introduction, Table of Contents, acknowledgements, copyright and credits page, etc. The back matter includes index, endnotes, About the Author, a blank page, and other options you may select for your book

☐ 2. The Book Cover: The book cover includes the front cover, which is an iconic representation of the content of the book; and the back cover, which includes a synopsis of the book and a bio of the author.

By the time you complete this simple project, you will have an awareness of all the pieces, parts, and components necessary and their order necessary to put a normal book together. Don't worry, we are providing the interior file of this book, so you won't have to worry about that part . . . at least not for now!

☐ **STEP 3**: Organize your Files.

I am going to save you hours of time and frustration right now! Listen to me. Start a new file folder. Name it MY BOOKS. Then create a new folder for each book project within this file folder. In the next step you will download a file we will provide for you. I am simplifying everything, so you can get through this process the first time. Once you successfully complete your book proof, you can move on to more advanced concepts; like creating your own interior book files. But that will come later. Let's keep it simple for now.

☐ **STEP 4**: Getting Your Book Blueprint Interior and Cover Files.

Go to www.publishingsolo.com/book-blueprint-template and download the interior and cover files, using the following password: ISBN-10: 061592171X. Save them to your file folder that you created in Step 3 called MY BOOKS.

☐ **STEP 5**: Sign-up for a POD Account.

POD stands for Print on Demand. In the digital publishing world, book files are created and saved; and when a book is ordered, that one book is printed from that file! No longer do 20,000 copies of one book need to be printed to make each book affordable. Printing one book at a time is affordable using digital printing. Now, this is where we are going to get you started in the learning the process, step by step.

Sign up for your personal print on demand account by pasting this link into the top of your brower: http://www.anrdoezrs.net/click-7230321-10801874. Once you complete the sign up process, they will send you a link to your email address which you will need to verify by clicking on the link they send to you. This is the wholesale printing arm for Amazon.com, the largest POD and online book distribution system in the world. Save your login and password information. You will need it soon.

☐ **STEP 6**: Create Your Book Cover.

Before we get started using Cover Creator on Createspace, I want to give you three tips how to make any book cover look professional; and not self-published.

1. Author name: Most self-published authors make the mistake of making their name too small on the cover of the book. Be bold, and make your book look like a best seller! Be sure the author name is large on the front of the book.

2. Graphic Elements: Whatever the image on the front cover of the book, be sure that it is a large bold graphic element. Most books are sold online, and your book cover will show up as a small icon; make it graphically striking.

3. Fonts: Use fonts that are not common. Most self-published authors are not creative with the use of fonts. Stay away from Times New Roman, or Ariel. Do some research and select fonts that are uncommon and have some style.

To get you through this process, we are going to use the Cover Creator online software provided by Createspace. Later, if you like you may hire someone to design a professional book cover, but for now, the idea of this course is to get your through the digital book publishing process for the first time.

Go to Createspace and login, if you have not done so already. At Member Dashboard, click on

1. The title of your book project. Look for set up at the top of your screen and click on "Cover," the fourth item down.

2. Next, you will select if you want a matt cover or a glossy cover.

3. And on the same screen, click on "Build Your Cover Online." Next you will click "Launch Cover Creator" at the bottom of the screen.

4. You'll see many book cover templates from which to choose; so select one you like. Don't worry, you can change it and it is fun to experiment.

5. The main thing is to practice. So click on a template you like and start playing around. You may use images for your front cover provided by Cover Creator or you may upload your own from your computer.

6. Complete 11 tasks as instructed by Cover Creator on the left side of screen. Upload author headshot, write a bio, synopsis, and select a cover photo.

7. Click on" Submit Cover," and you may edit or preview your book cover, prior to submitting your cover files for review.

8. If you have any questions with Cover Creator, contact Createspace for support.

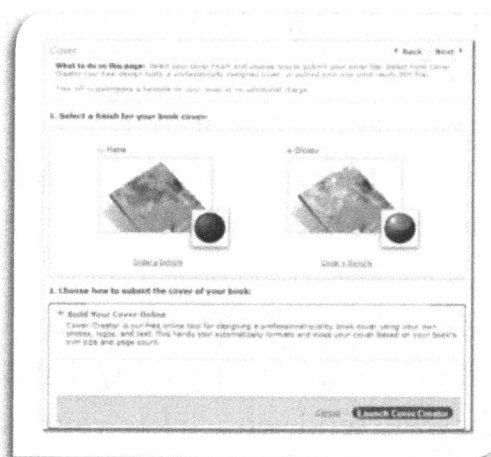

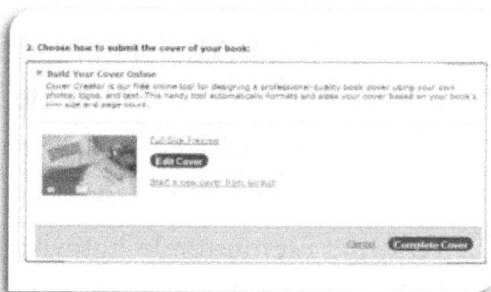

☐ **STEP 7**: Initiate Your Book Title.

1. Go to www.createspace.com and log in to your account with your user name and password and click on Member Dashboard. Click on the blue button that says "Add New Title."

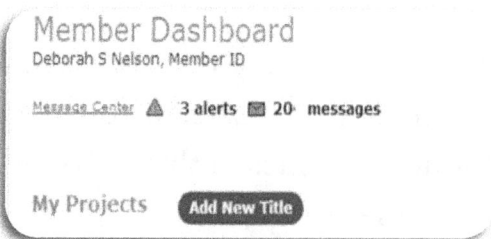

Member Dashboard
Deborah S Nelson, Member ID

Message Center ⚠ 3 alerts ✉ 20 messages

My Projects   Add New Title

2. Next window type in the title and subtitle of your book. Click on "Paperback," and "Guided Setup Process." Click on button that says "Get Started."

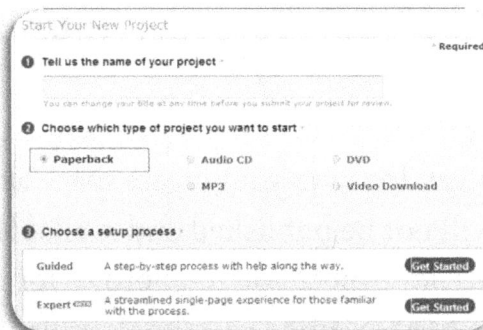

3. To keep it simple, in this next window, simply fill in the title of your book, subtitle, and your Author Name. This must be exactly the same as it appears in the interior of the book; and the book cover. If there is variation you will get an email from Createspace saying that they will not print it until these elements are consistent. Click Save and Continue button at the lower bottom right.

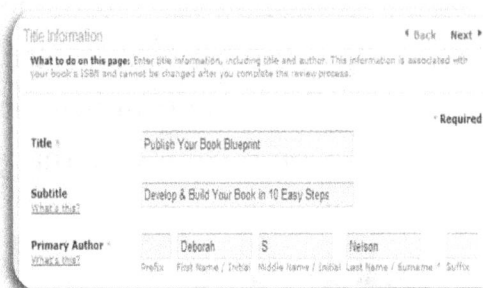

4. To keep it simple, so we can get you through this first round, simply select the Free Createspace-Assigned ISBN Number option. Click on Assign New ISBN button at the lower bottom right.

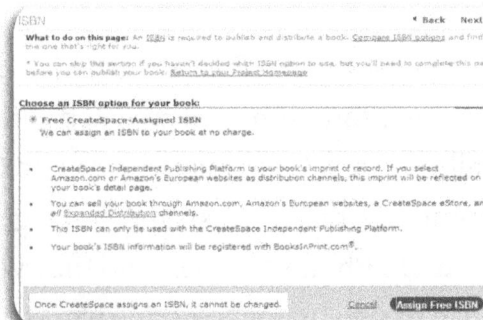

5. You will be assigned the ISBN (International Standard Book Number) and a screen will pop up with your ISBN number. Write down your ISBN numbers and save. Click "Continue."

6. Next screen, select size of your book, the color of the interior pages, either white or cream. The default size is 6" x 9", and you'll click on "Choose a Different Size" and choose 8.5 x 11. Your cover is designed as 8.5" x 11" and interior template is 8.5" x 11" as well. Click on "Ends after the end of the page," in the section that says "bleed." this is just below the window where you can upload your interior template. Go to your MY BOOKS file in your computer to upload the template entitled BOOKBLUEPRINTTEMPLATE.pdf

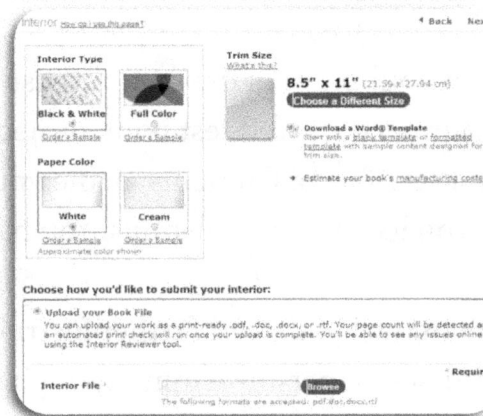

☐ **STEP 8**: Upload Your Book Cover

While your interior file is uploading, you will be given the option to upload your book cover. Follow the prompts and upload your book cover that you created using Cover Creator. Follow the instructions and click on the button that says "Submit Files for Review."

☐ **STEP 9**: Order Your Book Blueprint

You will be notified by CreateSpace in an email that your files have been approved for printing. Next, log in to your create space account. You will have an opportunity to order a proof. The book will not be published and available on AMAZON.Com for sale until you approve your proof. We do not expect you to approve your proof, but you can order a proof and use the test book journal to further refine your book project. Once you receive your proof, the book file will sit in Amazon. com until you approve the proof for publication. Of course, we do not suggest you do this, because this is only a sample book so you can learn about the process. When you are ready with your book project, you'll initiate your own title, and upload your own interior. After you receive the proof of your book, you can approve that proof and <u>Createspace</u> will publish it and make it available on Amazon.com for sale.

☐ **STEP 10**: Prepare for Final Publication

A NOTE ABOUT APPROVAL: I have super-simplified this process for you. But, in digital publishing there are sometimes unexpected glitches. If your file is not approved for some unexpected reason, simply call or email Customer Service at Createspace. Have your PROJECT ID and Createspace account number, email address, and you'll get all the help you need. Go to the contact support area and type in your US Phone number; and they will call you back immediately If this is too difficult for you, you may wish to sign up for an online workshop at PublishingSOLO.com.

Get your proof in the mail and use your Book Blueprint Journal to fine tune, organize and write in your personalized test book project. Fill in the Title of Your Book Project. Write your dedication. In the Table of Contents, name your chapters. Write your chapters in the journal area of the book, if you like. Congratulations. You have now completed the process of uploading a book to Amazon.

If you feel you need further instruction, you may register for any of the Publishing SOLO online courses, in person seminars, or private publishing coaching with Deborah S. Nelson.

Now that you have completed your book blueprint, you are qualified for a complimentary half hour of publishing coaching with Deborah S. Nelson. Go to www.PublishingSOLO.com and click on Publishing Coaching at the top menu. Look for the Complimentary Coaching Session link in the drop down menu.

PART II

BOOK BLUEPRINT JOURNAL

FRONT MATTER

Front matter introduces your book to your readers. It includes preliminary information such as the book's title page, the name of its publisher and copyrights. The front matter section appears before the body of the book and consists of preliminary pages such as the preface, foreword and acknowledgements. Identify which of the typical front matter pages are suitable for your book. If your book is particularly scholarly or detailed you may also include such pages as Abbreviations, List of Images, or anything else which would further set the stage for the rest of the book.

Notes:

INSTRUCTIONS

Organize your book interior here, or create your own with your custom book cover and published book blueprint by using the steps in Chapter 5.

This workbook serves 2 purposes. You can use this section as your generic blueprint to write and prepare your book for print on demand publishing. This Book Blueprint method will help you publish your book to Amazon.com using Createspace, the wholesale printing division of Amazon.

Or, you can use the instructions to customize and personalize your Book Blueprint as given in Chapter 5. Either way, you will use the interior section that follows to complete the interior details of the book. This is a workbook, and it would be such a crime if you did not write in it.

Notes: _____

_____

_____

_____

_____

_____

_____

_____

PRAISE FOR_____

(Title of the Book)

These are the very first pages of the book; and is often used to include quotes from those who have read and reviewed the book and have wonderful things to say.

_____

_____

_____

_____

_____

_____

_____

_____

_____

_____

HALF TITLE PAGE

TITLE HERE: _____

Book half title; write the title of your book here. Be sure it is exactly how it is listed in the title you will create in your print on demand account. You may also include your subtitle.

_____
Subtitle

_____
Author Name

BLANK

(this page is blank in order to cause the following page to be on the odd numbered right side of the book)

SERIES TITLE, FRONTSPIECE, OR BLANK

If this is a series, write your series title here.

_____

_____

_____

_____

_____

BLANK

(this page is blank in order to cause the following page to be on the odd numbered right side of the book)

TITLE PAGE

Your title and subtitle go here along with a logo or interior design illustration.

_____

Title

_____

Subtitle

_____

Author Name

COPYRIGHT PAGE

```
LOGO
PUBLILSHING
COMPANY
(OPTIONAL)
```

DEDICATION

Use this area to dedicate your book to whomever.

_____

_____

_____

_____

_____

_____

_____

BLANK

(this page is blank in order to cause the following page to be on the odd numbered right side of the book)

EPIGRAPH

A quotation set at the beginning of a literary work to suggest its theme.

_____

_____

_____

_____

_____

_____

_____

BLANK

(this page is blank in order to cause the following page to be on the odd numbered right side of the book)

TABLE OF CONTENTS

LIST OF ILLUSTRATIONS

(Optional)

LIST OF TABLES

(Optional)

_____

_____

_____

_____

_____

_____

_____

_____

_____

_____

_____

FOREWORD

A foreword is a stamp of approval on the book; a recommendation most often written by someone other than the author who is an expert in the field that the book will cover. Forewords are a marketing tool, and we hope for an opening statement by a celebrity or well-known author which gives the author credibility and a tool to market the book.

_____

_____

_____

_____

_____

_____

_____

_____

_____

_____

_____

PREFACE

The author can use the preface to explain why they are qualified to write the book. Taking an outside look at the book, the author explains briefly why they wrote the book, or what inspired them to write it. Authors can use the preface to establish credibility, and as a platform to persuade why the reader should heed their words; and how the author is qualified to write on the topic. It is a continuation of the foreword, but written by the author.

_____

_____

_____

_____

_____

_____

_____

_____

_____

ACKNOWLEDGMENTS

Appreciate those who inspired you and helped you with the details of putting this book together:

_____

_____

_____

_____

_____

_____

_____

_____

_____

_____

_____

_____

_____

BLANK

(this page is blank in order to cause the following page to be on the odd numbered right side of the book)

INTRODUCTION

Explain what your book is about; and why you wrote it and why you are qualified to write it. The introduction is a more detailed discussion about the content of the book and how it can be used. The Introduction sets the overall theme of the book, by establishing definitions and methodology being used throughout the book. The Introduction can explain how the book is organized, and the best ways to understand and apply the material. Sometimes, you can confuse the introduction and the preface; but keep in mind, the Foreword represents a bigger picture, how it fits into a bigger scope. The Preface moves in a little closer to describe the need for the book, and the Introduction explains the details of how to apply or understand the organization of the book.

_____

_____

_____

_____

_____

_____

_____

_____

_____

ABBREVIATIONS

(if not in the back matter)

_____

_____

_____

_____

_____

_____

_____

_____

_____

_____

_____

_____

CHRONOLOGY

(if not in the back matter)

_____

_____

_____

_____

_____

_____

_____

_____

_____

_____

_____

_____

BLANK

(this page is blank in order to cause the following page to be on the odd numbered right side of the book)

BODY OF BOOK

<u>EXPLANATION OF THE BODY OF THE BOOK:</u>
The text in the center or body of the book includes the narrative—including arguments, data, illustrations, photos, charts, graphs, etc.—divided into chapters and other organizational sections.

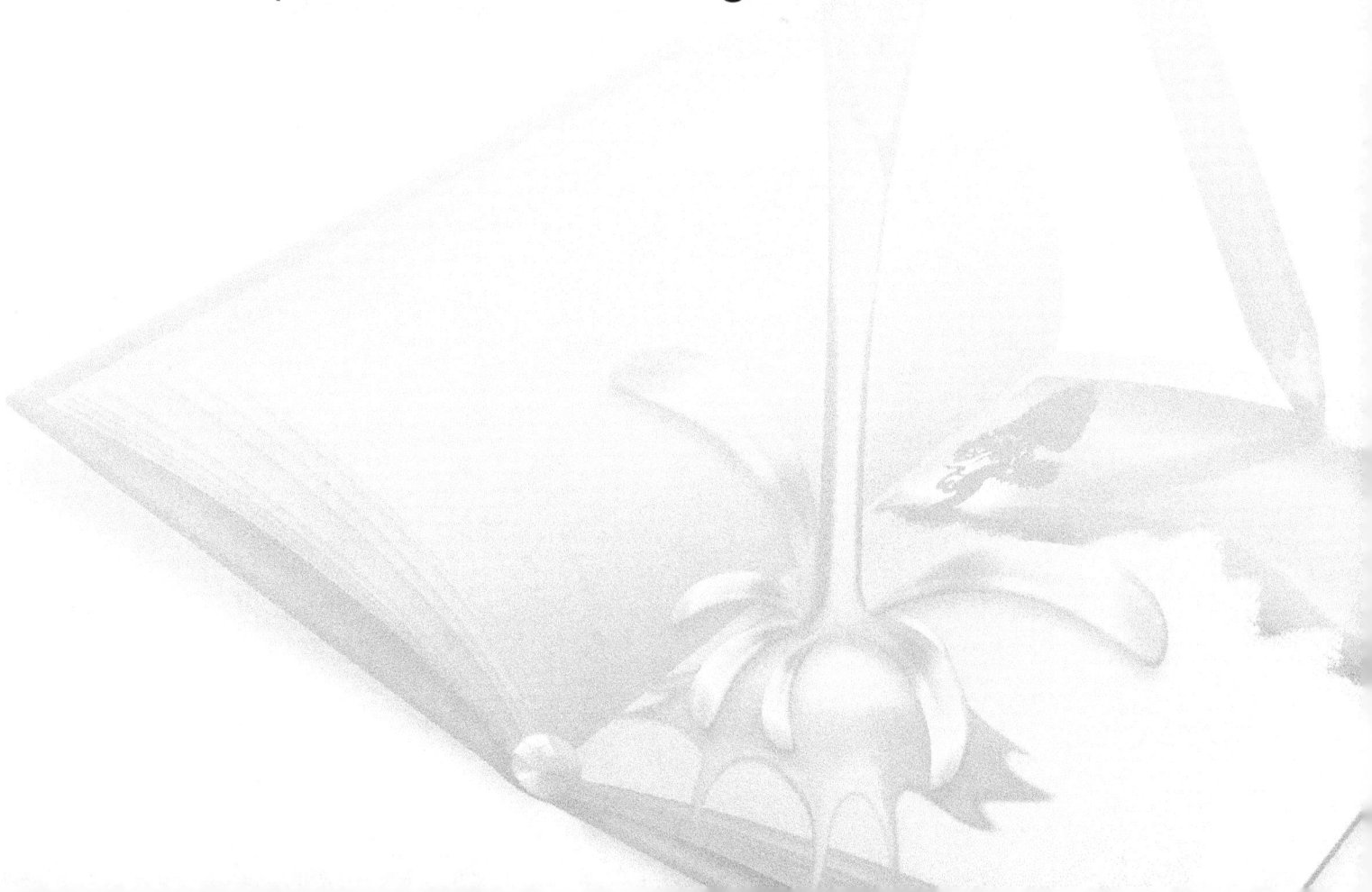

BLANK

(this page is blank in order to cause the following page to be on the odd numbered right side of the book)

HALF TITLE PAGE

Second Half Title or First Part Title

_____

Title

_____

Subtitle

_____

Author Name

BLANK

(this page is blank in order to cause the following page to be on the odd numbered right side of the book)

CHAPTER 1 TITLE: _____

_____

_____

_____

_____

_____

_____

_____

_____

_____

_____

_____

_____

_____

_____

_____

CHAPTER 2 TITLE:_____

CHAPTER 3 TITLE:_____

_____
_____
_____
_____
_____
_____
_____
_____
_____
_____
_____
_____
_____
_____

CHAPTER 4 TITLE:_____

CHAPTER 5 TITLE: _____

_____

_____

_____

_____

_____

_____

_____

_____

_____

_____

_____

_____

_____

_____

CHAPTER 6 TITLE: _____

_____

_____

_____

_____

_____

_____

_____

_____

_____

_____

_____

_____

_____

_____

_____

CHAPTER 7 TITLE: _____

CHAPTER 8 TITLE:_____

CHAPTER 9 TITLE: _____

CHAPTER 10 TITLE: _____

CHAPTER 11 TITLE:_____

CHAPTER 12 TITLE: _____

CHAPTER 13 TITLE: _____

CHAPTER 14 TITLE: _____

_____

_____

_____

_____

_____

_____

_____

_____

_____

_____

_____

_____

_____

_____

_____

CHAPTER 15 TITLE: _____

CHAPTER 16 TITLE: _____

BACK MATTER

BACK MATTER EXPLANATION:

The back matter includes sources or resources, appendixes, and other documentation supporting the premise or content of the book, but outside its main point. The back matter can include such things as a dictionary of terms, further resources, bibliography, endnotes, and further information to elaborate and support the concept of the book.

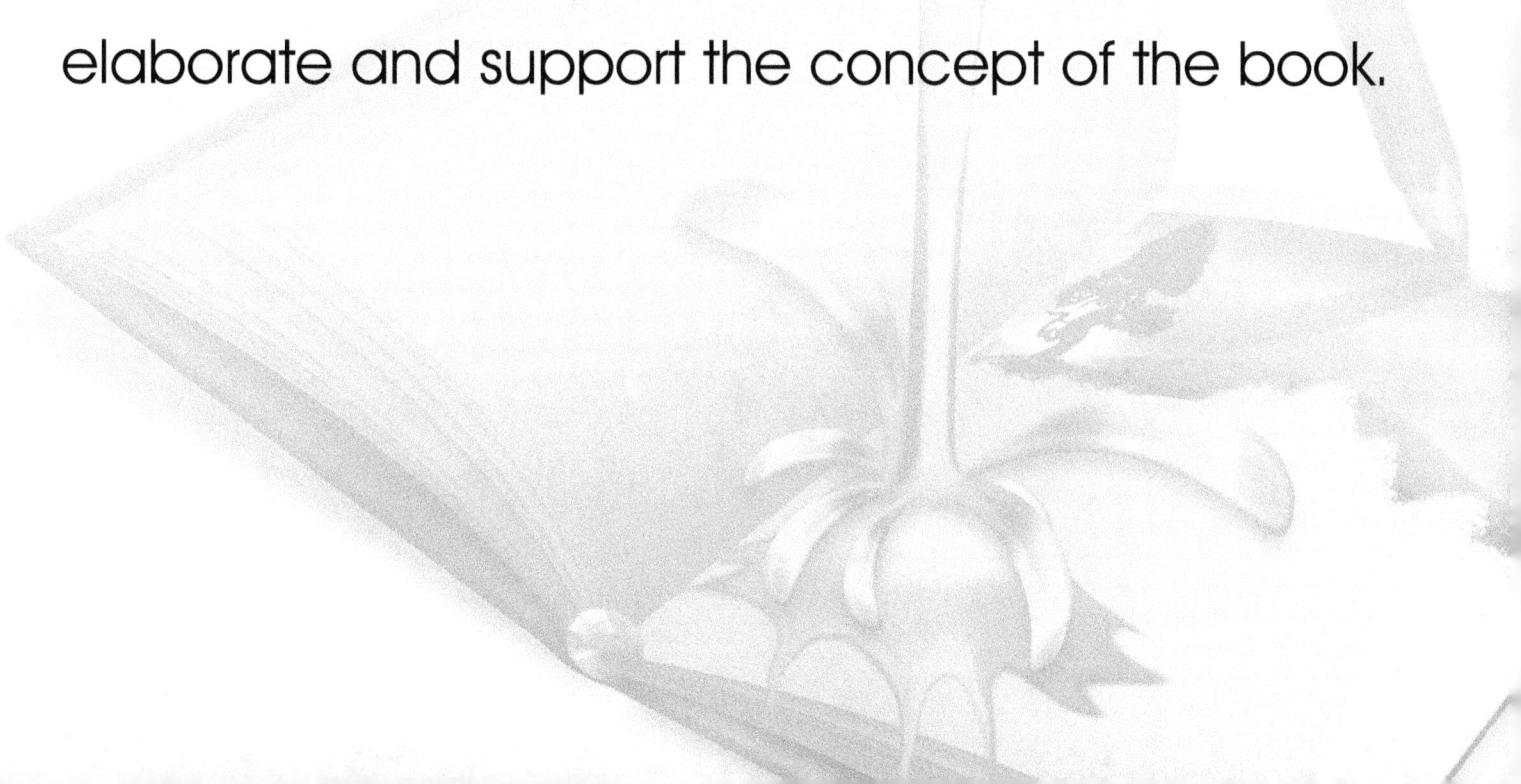

BLANK

(this page is blank in order to cause the following page to be on the odd numbered right side of the book)

APPENDIX

(or first appendix, if more than one)

_____

_____

_____

_____

_____

_____

_____

_____

_____

_____

_____

_____

SECOND AND SUBSEQUENT APPENDIXES

(Optional)

CHRONOLOGY

(if not in front matter)

ABBREVIATIONS

(if not in front matter)

217

NOTES

GLOSSARY

BIBLIOGRAPHY OR REFERENCES

LIST OF CONTRIBUTORS

ILLUSTRATION CREDITS

(if not in captions or elsewhere)

_____

_____

_____

_____

_____

_____

_____

_____

_____

_____

_____

_____

INDEXES

The index is an alphabetically ordered list of terms used for referencing your text.

_____

_____

_____

_____

_____

_____

_____

_____

_____

_____

_____

_____

BLANK

(this page is blank in order to cause the following page to be on the odd numbered right side of the book)

ABOUT THE AUTHOR

BLANK

(this page is blank in order to cause the following page to be on the odd numbered right side of the book)

OTHER BOOKS & SERVICES BY AUTHOR

(other books and a description of courses, consulting services, contact info, websites, etc.)

BLANK

(this page is blank in order to cause the following page to be on the odd numbered right side of the book)

About the Author

Dreaming and Writing—What do they have in common? Perhaps it is Deborah S. Nelson—who has united her two greatest talents within her recent book series, *Author Your Reality ACTION PLAN*.

Her ability to guide dreams to reality inspired Ms. Nelson to invent and author this unique three-part learning series—the first of its kind!

The author's first big dream, at 14, was to become a newspaper editor and writer. And she fulfilled that dream early on, within her first year of junior high school.

Photography by
Jamie Nelson

Her next dream was to fund her college education. Still in love with writing, between studies and work she made time to write for her college newspaper. Dreaming and writing, she graduated in the 70s, debt free, with a BS from the University of Texas. Soon after, she joined *The Austin Sun,* a weekly entertainment and cultural magazine.

In the '80s, Ms. Nelson emerged from a difficult divorce in the role of *sole functioning parent*. This challenge created just one thing for Nelson, a new dream—to raise her daughter as a happy, healthy, successful person, rather than as another statistic of a broken home.

Concern for her child's future propelled her into a new era and a new dream-to start one of the first "home-based businesses." That dream realized gave her freedom to be a full-time, *on-purpose, solo mom.*

Eventually, Nelson was able to fund most of her daughter's education at Brooks Institute of Photography, her daughter's dream college!

Devoted to women in business, Nelson was recognized by *Working Women Magazine* in the '90s for entrepreneurial excellence; and selected as a national finalist for Ms. Corporate America 2008—another childhood dream realized. In 2013, Nelson was nominated for the THE AMERICAN RIVIERA WOMAN ENTREPRENEUR OF THE YEAR, with a focus to celebrate woman who are change-agents globally. As Nelson seeks to infiltrate the globe with dream-doers, this is her most exciting recognition to date.

In the *Author Your Reality Action Plan,* a synthesis of 25 years of study, reading, and life experience, Nelson masterfully merges two recurring themes—her love of writing, and her ability to set dreams in motion. What is her next big dream? Her dream is to teach millions of readers how to write and publish their dream book and bring their dreams to reality!

You may contact Deborah S. Nelson for private publishing coaching or online publishing courses at *www.PublishingSOLO.com* or email her at *dnelson@PublishingSOLO.com*

Other Books by Deborah S. Nelson

* All Books Available on Amazon.com

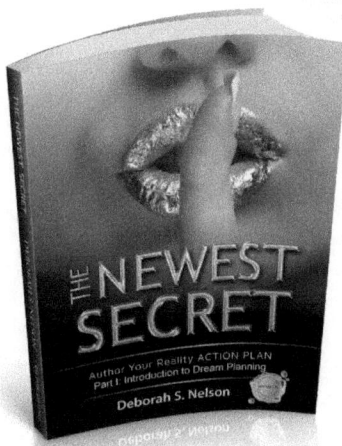

www.TheNewestSecret.com

www.TheNewestSecret.com

www.TheNewestSecret.com

www.TheNewestSecret.com

www.TheVacationRentalGuide.com

www.TheVacationRentalGuide.com

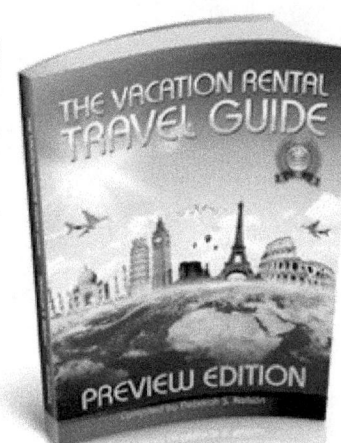

www.TheVacationRentalGuide.com

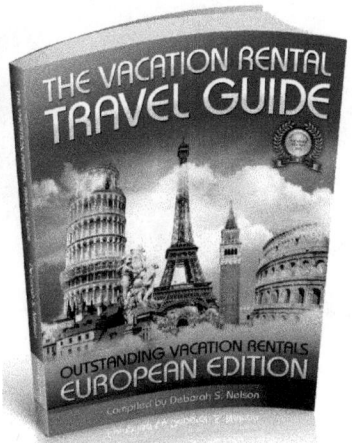

www.TheVacationRentalGuide.com

Other Inspired Living Books

* All Books Available on Amazon.com

www.daretodetoxify.com   www.TheFreshFoodChef.com   www.TheFreshFoodChef.com   www.rippleeffectgame.com

www.OvertheEdgePublishing.com   www.OvertheEdgePublishing.com   www.GameShiftPress.com

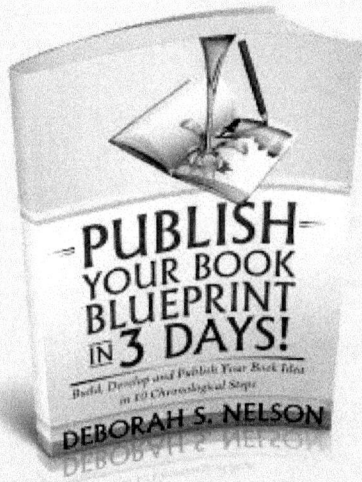

Do You Have aDream to Publish a Book— But Lack the Time or Know-How?

Look no further. This powerful learn-by-doing guide grants you the time and know-how. Learn to publish a printed book in 3 days by actually doing it! Once you become a published author, your friends, family, and peers will see you in a whole new light! This unique new system teaches both aspiring and seasoned authors every step of the self-publishing process. _You won't even need your completed manuscript to get started_. This Book Blueprint system:

- ❧ **Includes a downloadable interior template**
- ❧ **Displays parts of a book in chronological order**
- ❧ **Gives 10 easy steps to print on demand publishing**
- ❧ **Sets up free ISBN number and self-publishing account**
- ❧ **Gets your blueprint published in 3 days! (shipping extra)**

Want to learn how to publish a book in 3 days?

Go to http://www.publishingsolo.com/book-blueprint-course-order-2/

END SHEET